Collection of Poetry
by
Sandy Robinson

in Memory of Sandy Robinson
and for all our family and friends

ISBN 0 9520486 0 4

Printed by W. & G. Baird Ltd., Antrim

Collection of Poetry
by
Sandy Robinson

The Bard of Ballyalbanagh

Illustrated by Joanne Robinson
Introduction by Jack McKinney

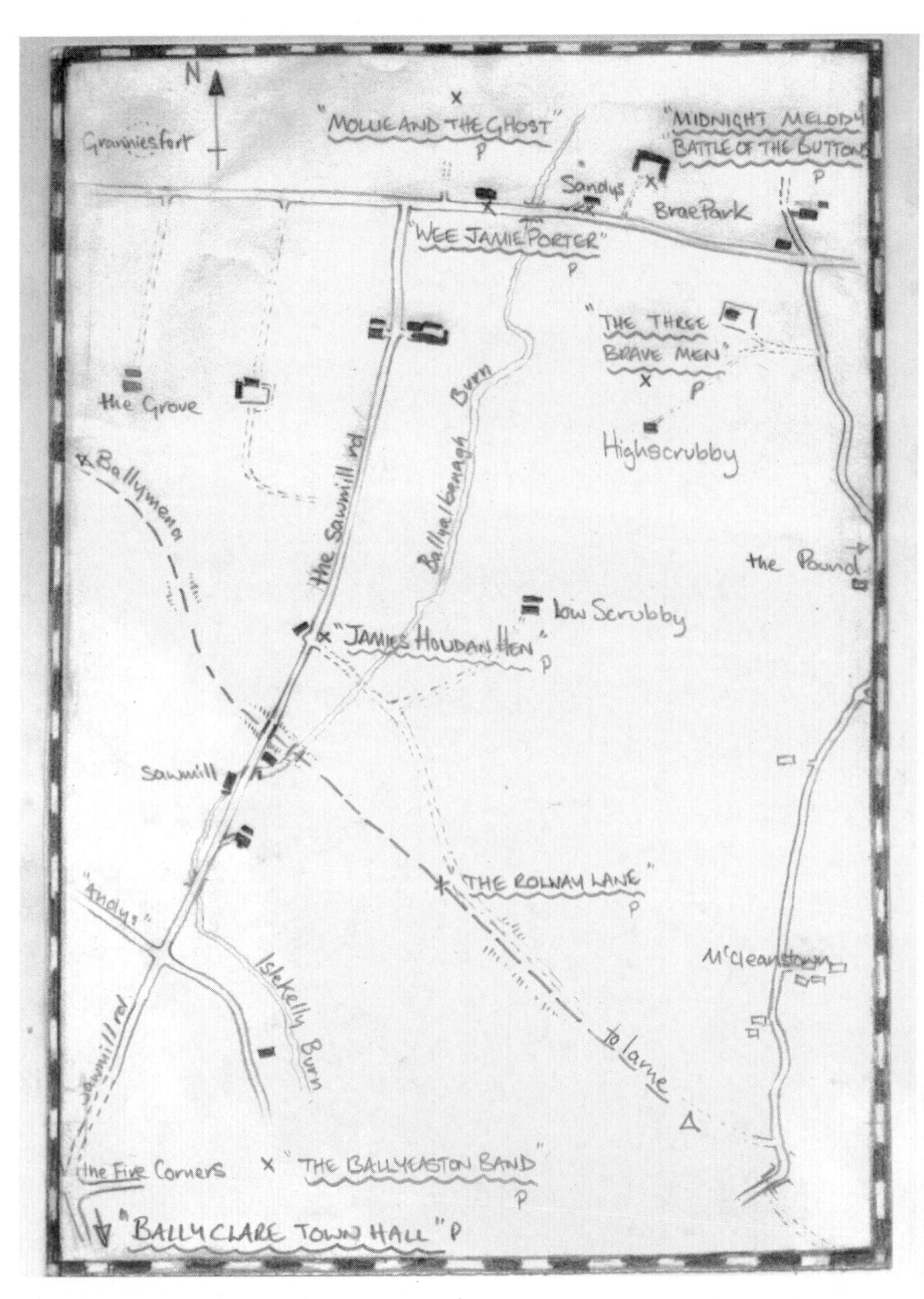
N
"MOLLIE AND THE GHOST"
P
"MIDNIGHT MELODY"
BATTLE OF THE BUTTONS
P
Granniesfort
Sandys
BraePark
"WEE JAMIE PORTER"
P
"THE THREE BRAVE MEN"
P
the Grove
Highscrubby
Ballymena
the Sawmill rd
Ballyalbanagh Burn
the Pound
low Scrubby
"JAMIES HOUDAN HEN"
P
Sawmill
"THE ROLWAY LANE"
P
"Andys"
Isle Kelly Burn
M'Cleanstown
Sawmill rd
to Larne
the Five Corners
"THE BALLYEASTON BAND"
P
"BALLYCLARE TOWN HALL" P

INTRODUCTION

Alexander McGladdery Robinson was born on 11 September 1910, the seventh child of Thomas John and Eliza Jane (nee Hill) in a family of nine. He was named after a very good friend of his father.

Their hill farm home at Braepark was not large and times were hard, but school and church were attended regularly and the difference between right and wrong was taught at their mother's knee.

When their chores were done, they made their own fun, footballing, tramping, playing chequers and boxing. The older brothers sang in the church choir and taught themselves to play musical instruments. Samuel, Sandy and Jack joined Ballyboley Pipe Band and Jack and Sandy played the violin, with Sandy going on to do well in fiddling competitions.

That was when they weren't going to dances or playing at them, walking or, as he says in the poem 'Oul Age', getting Matt Meharg to take them farther afield in his car.

'The Mester', page 33, was a frequent visitor in their home, enjoying Thomas John's crack, and a game of chequers, page 31, as in a 'Battle wi' Buttons.' Master McAllister was a great influence in Sandy's life at Ballynashee School and had further education been possible, who knows what he would have done.

As it was, hard work at the butchering, which all the brothers went into, Sam in Carrickfergus, Robert in Larne and Sandy in Ballyclare (where they all started out), enabled them to set up their own homes. Some with Sandy's help as he had then gone into building and had a hand in many renovations, barns, sheds, and bungalows around the countryside. Jean took a great interest in all this and while creating their own home helped in plans for others, including our own and her niece, Lylas.

There wasn't much enthusiasm left in him for creating poems after his beloved Jean died, page 97. They had had such a good life together. Their picnics and outings to view the orchards of Armagh in spring and the changing colours of the trees in autumn, often included their many nephews and nieces. Fond memories of these trips are treasured by those who enjoyed them and their visits to their home and Braepark.

His parents were everything to him and in their later years when his mother was confined to an armchair by the fire she kept them on the right lines and cleaned all their boots and shoes. The family they reared were a credit to them and they would have been well pleased if they had been spared to see them all established in life, page 95, 'To my father on his death bed'.

Sadness and illness touched their growing years when Lizzie died at seventeen after getting a soaking going to a dance, page 82, 'On the death of a sister'. Then when Jack took rheumatic fever, page 70, 'A Prayer for Jack' was written. Then 'a Toast' to Robert and Marie on their wedding day, page 85, brought in happier times. He was very close to his sisters, Mary, Rachel, Jeannie and Sadie. Letters to Rachel, page 86, in Southport and later Bristol were common. The poem written on the death of King George V was sent to Queen Mary and her lady-in-waiting kindly wrote back, thanking Sandy for his verses.

Many of these I read and recited at church and school concerts.

After I graduated from fashion college in England and moved to Paris, in my summer at home I tried to illustrate Sandy's poems as I had always dreamed of doing as a little girl. He was such a special man, so humble: this book would have never been printed in his lifetime. He wanted to share his humour and thoughts with everyone in poems and I'll always remember how impressed I was that he ate all my mud pies in my tree house, and left a tip! Then when I grew up I recited his poems at concerts, etc.

I know Ballyalbanagh and all of County Antrim is a treasure in both of our eyes. As artists we see the beauty in the land that in everyday life, others forget. I hope this book takes you out into our countryside. Walk where Sandy walked and wrote poetry and where I've followed and drawn our townland, glens and monuments.

I hope he would have been happy with the actual book design. I'd also like to thank Jack McKinney for his help and guidance, my Granny Robinson for advice and spelling check and my Mother for liaising with the printers while I've been away.

Joanne Robinson

CONTENTS

	Page
Ballyclare Town Hall	1
Ballymena Painter	2
Carrickfergus Castle	4
To the Emerald Isle	7
The Glasgow Exhibition	9
The Rolway Lane	11
The Hills and Dells of Antrim	12
Ballyeaston Band	14
Kathleen	17
An Irish Immigrant	18
A Pretty Country Maid	19
Answer to a Proposal	20
Congratulations	21
At Eventide	22
Lorna Doon	23
The Faithful Lover	24
A Disappointment	25
In Loneliness	27
A Scholar's Lament	28
A Battle wi' Buttons	30
The Mester	33
The Duke of Windsor	36
The Three Brave Men	38
Bonnie Gertie	40
Mollie and the Ghost	41
A Drunkard	43
St. Patrick	45
Wee Jamie Porter	47
My Mother	48
The Mountain Terrace	50
The Highway Code	52
King George V	54
The Ulster LDV	55
The Crisis	57
Peace in Ballyclare	58
Oul Age	59
Hard Times	60
To Robert	62
A Midnight Melody	63
A Poacher's Lament	65
On a Victim of Scarlet Fever	66
Tryst	67
Mrs McIntyre Goes to Kirk	68
A Prayer for Jack	70
A Child	71
The Holy Land	72
The Shepherd and His Sheep	73
To a Sister with a Xmas Card	74
The Potter and the Clay	75
Appeals from the Church	77
The Pope's Visit to Ireland	78
A Meditation	81
On the Death of a Sister	82
A Prayer	83
A Toast	85
A Letter to Ray in Southport	86
To James McCrory	88
An Apology	89
A Consoling Recitation	90
A Bereavement	91
To a Robin	92
A Prayer	94
To My Father on His Death	95
Drawing of His Wife	96
Jean	97

Sadly I came to know Sandy Robinson much too late in his life. When I moved to Tildarg in 1978 and it became known that I was interested in local history and folklore I was often told that I would have to go over to Ballyalbanagh to see Sandy. Eventually one Friday night I knocked on his door. I was warmly welcomed and brought in to a seat beside the fire. It was well past midnight when I returned to Tildarg, my head bizzing with Sandy's stories. That night and after many subsequent Friday visits I startled my wife by laughing aloud in my sleep, an understandable reaction to his skill in telling witty yarns and anecdotes. Television was never a serious rival to Sandy.

He was a superb mimic and could reproduce almost exactly the mannerisms, facial expressions and, indeed, the tone of voice of all the many eccentric characters he had met in the district. Somewhat shy of performing in public in his latter days he then much preferred to remain a fireside entertainer but in earlier years he regularly played the fiddle and accordion at socials and dances throughout the country. Also a member of the Collin Ceilidhe Band he had a fund of good stories about his experiences on the local entertainment circuit.

Sandy took an active part for many years in the popular custom of Christmas rhyming and with friends from Ballyboley he tramped the fields and lanes often through gutters to the knee and usually braving savage dogs to bring these exotic plays to country homes not always entirely glad to welcome the motley band. On one occasion the party featured on a BBC radio programme with Sandy talking about this seasonal pursuit. Their fee then far exceeded the more modest total of their usual collections but the treat it provided was no more precious than in one particular year when their money was used to buy a 'bladder' ball for the Ballyalbanagh football team, the Yett Brae Blargers.

Sandy had a variety of jobs in his time from butcher to working in the building trade. He was popular with his customers for his wit and there were building jobs prolonged by clients simply to hear more of Sandy's crack. While doing renovations in houses he often found old documents or discarded newspapers which fed his natural interest in any aspect of the past. His house contained an extensive collection of tattered books, wills and maps and he had become a recognised authority on the lineage of many families in the district. His own ancestors had arrived as very early settlers in Ballyalbanagh, the townland of the Scots.

At week-ends he was often to be seen dandering over his native fields, examining caves, mounds and forts supplying the inspiration for fascinating theories about life in ancient times on these braes. His local knowledge proved useful to the archaeologists carrying out a survey in these uplands and they proved the accuracy of his information through their subsequent excavations.

But those who recognised his many talents judged his poems to be his best accomplishment. He had a natural sense of rhyme, his acute observation and detailed knowledge of the countryside combined with his ability to describe odd incidents and the unusual characters of the district made Sandy Robinson a formidable poet indeed. The verse also portrays different moods from the humorous to the contemplative with a poignant sadness pervading some poems, a creditable range indeed from someone who had not the benefit of an extensive formal education. Above all, too, there is a sensitivity and sympathy for his subjects, especially for those who had suffered misfortune in life.

He had the distinction, rare for an unpublished poet, of having some of his verses quoted in *The Irish Times*. They charmed the late Eileen O'Brien on a visit to Ballyclare in 1984 and she chose to include some lines in her weekly column 'An Irishwoman's Diary' some weeks later.

All his life Sandy had a deep love for nature and he spent much time in his garden especially in spring and summer. He was fond of listening to the birds and they seemed to know of his affection for them because they nested in the most peculiar places around his home. He had a tape recording of his brood singing and this consoled him when the changing seasons brought silence.

Sandy Robinson died in 1986 and was buried in Rashee cemetery where fourteen years earlier his dear wife Jean had been laid to rest. Their headstone there appropriately has on it an inscription of two lines from a poem written by Sandy as a tribute to Jean:

> The flowers, the sunsets, the tints on a tree
> Were glimpses of heaven to Jeanie and me.

Visitors to the grave will sometimes tell you that the birds sing more sweetly in this part of the cemetery than in any other. Now that's the kind of tribute Sandy and Jean would really have appreciated.

This fine book of verse will surely stir a wealth of memories among his many friends and give a lot of pleasure both to them and others who have not previously heard of Sandy Robinson, the Bard of Ballyalbanagh.

Jack McKinney
12 September 1992

THE BALLYCLARE TOWN HALL
Nov 1992

'The Ballyclare Town Hall'

There may be buildings built for style
   Adorned wi' different kins
O' ornamental images
   An' fancy work designs
But should you search the "Emerald Isle"
   From Cork to Donegal
You wou'dny see a structure like
   The Ballyclare Town Hall.

It stan's for no particular cause
   Nor differs its desires
But lends alike its massive space
   For what the town requires.
To business, pleasure, or to prayer
   To all things great an' small
The door is ever open at
   The Ballyclare Town Hall.

The Yankees usually blow an' boast
   How they can build so high
And where their towers terminate
   A fraction from the sky.
An' sure enough the world admits
   That Yankees make 'em tall
But not so huge and splendid as
   The Ballyclare Town Hall.

A stranger passing through the town
   A Beggar, or an Earl
Would stop and gaze as if it were
   A wonder o' this worl'
An' even when folk from far and near
   Forgather at a ball
They canny dance for glowering at
   The Ballyclare Town Hall.

The Duke o' York once crossed by air
   From London to Stranraer
And on its route the Royal plane
   Passed over Ballyclare.
On peepin' out the Duke exclaimed
   Behold the courts of Saul
Oh, nonsense, says the pilot, that's
   The Ballyclare Town Hall.

He talked about his Da and Ma
He meant the King and Queen
If they could only cross the sea
An' see what he had seen.
But sure if they, their Majesties,
Would see the place atall
They would bring their Royal flittin tae'
The Ballyclare Town Hall.

So if you're fond of seeing sights
That never lea' your eyes
Just come and get a glimpse of what
This masterpiece supplies.
An' should you never see again
You'll say 'twas worth it all
E'en just to have it said you saw
The Ballyclare Town Hall.

The Ballymena Painter

I know a boy, ca'd Roy McCloy, a painter frae the Toon,
Whose skill and fame hae made his name renowned for miles aroon.
His gifted hands like magic wands propelled him to a class
That only Michaelangelo was privileged to surpass.

He had aye a taste for paint 'n paste, and when he finished school
He left the Braid to learn the trade, wi' Terrence P. O'Tool.
The brush and pot would be his lot, and some day he'd succeed
Except perchance that Providence had otherwise decreed.

Without a friend, nor cash to spend on 'Pictures', chips or 'cigs'.
He'd do odd jobs for twothree bob to help to pay his digs.
He'd gether bins o' crusts and skins for Molly McIlveen
Or boil a can of "Yellowman" for 'Ballymena Jean'.

And yet tho' poor and insecure his promise he maintained
Thro' five long years of hopes and fears, and never once complained.
But served O'Tool his time in full, learned all about the trade
The tips and tricks on what to mix for any special shade.

Now on his own, he works alone, resolved to do his best
To execute what best would suit each customer's request.
No job too small, no house too tall, no type of work refused;
No dirt, no draps, no ugly japs, nor furniture abused.

A sash that leaks, a door that creaks, his hand will soon repair
Unflinching spots like cracks and knots you'd swear were never there.
Around hinges, locks and "Cuckoo clocks", behind a curtain rail,
He'll cover joints and awkward points where other painters fail.

In spite of breed, belief or creed, alike to rich and poor
He'll varnish gates on big Estates, or prime a cottage door.
He'll paint a Church or glaze a porch for Moslems or Jews:
Distempter walls of Orange Halls or grain the Chapel pews.

In Temperance Clubs, in Village Pubs, he'll work with equal joy
The Preacher and the Publican are all the same to Roy;
A caravan in Magherabann; a donkey's cart in Cork;
Come heat or coul his heart and soul are always in his work.

The Toon will miss a man like this, when he receives the call
To join the best, the first and greatest Architect of all;
The shades he made may chip and fade, and vanish bye and bye,
But perhaps we'll see some bigger, brighter rainbows in the sky.

"Carrick Castle"

Carrick Castle

There's a very ancient castle built
  Upon the Irish coast
And few such structures of its day
  Could of its better boast.

A castle that existed through
  The sword and pistol age
Whose stalwart walls withstood the storm
  Of many a bitter siege.

'Twas there the Kings from foreign climes
  Took up their first abode
And each new heir took power from there
  To cast the laws abroad.

'Twas there the rebels of our race
  Their cruel sentence served
And many's a noble suffered there
  A scourge he ne'er deserved.

Since then the final Royal race
  From thence have passed away
And now the castle tells a tale
  Of ruin and decay.

All o'er the courtyard once so clean
  Now grows a grassy sod
To hide the prints where oft the feet
  Of gallant yeomen trod.

But years of absence and abuse
  The cause of change explain
As nature from the work of man
  Her lawful rights reclaim.

Tho' shattered by the hand of time
  This ruined frame displays
Sufficient evidence to prove
  Their skill in former days.

'Tis plainly seen that here has been
  A fortress well prepared
To render shelter and defence
  When battles were declared.

With guns to shield the shore front
When foes were nigh at hand
And walls to mar the men of war
That choose the solid land.

With tapered loop-holes through the walls
Providing space between
Where skilful bow and arrow men
Could see and not be seen.

Yet with its fearless fortitude
'Twould be a small debar
Against an aerial attack
In modern ways of war.

For science since is so advanced
It shadows ancient power
And overthrows the strength that once
O'ercame in danger's hour.

But for the sake of those who lived
In Erin's early days
'Tis sad that such a souvenir
Should moulder and decay.

For this a dwelling place for Kings
For Royalty designed
Where lofty Lords and Ladies danced
Where Dukes and Earls dined.

But, ah, no more the banquet hall
With mirth and music rings
No more to Kings an' Governors
The cheerful minstrel sings.

The rustic shell that clad those scenes
Is all that there remains
All sights and sounds have long resigned
And gloom an' silence reigns.

To The Emerald Isle

Where are the Bands, oh Emerald Isle,
That sympathise with thee?
And why so long their harps hang mute
Upon the willow tree?

As thou, unshielded, fast approach
Disaster's bending brink
I truly feel inclined to voice
The thought that thousands think.

I know thy burden's hard to bear,
The way thou'rt crushed 'tis cruel,
Thy Home Sweet Home fires have to burn
On far too little fuel.

How could a prosperous year revolve
Or happy homes exist
When hard wrought tillers of the soil
Are ruthlessly oppressed.

I think the men of church an' state
If such within them are
Have less regard for thee than for
The heathen from afar.

Oh, would some honest body rise
Ere civil wars grow rife
Who could conduct thy tide o' time
O'er the raging seas of life.

'Twould please thy discontented sons
To lease thy loyal gore
Who now by fortune's cruel storms
Are strewn on every shore.

Had I the pith o' Samson's power
Or Moses' pedigree
I'd drop the scythe this very hour
And gladly set them free.

With staff an' jaw bone I'd defend
My home, my native sod
I'd comb the Isle from end to end
An' cross the Boyne dry shod.

E'en could I rule, I'd massacre
The foe that first defies thee
But, ah, alas my aim falls short
As poverty denies me.

And oh, the humble strive in vain,
Who wordly schemes devise
When men o lordly pomp an' pride
The poor man's views despise.

Then here's my hope – that may the bud
Of brighter seasons bloom
An' may some distant dawning sun
Illuminate thy gloom.

The Glasgow Exhibition

From reading books and hearing yarns,
I got a foolish notion
That joy and beauty only lay
Beyond the briny ocean.
So just to please a wish that preyed
On my imagination
I joined a ship and took a trip
To see the Exhibition.

'Twas stormy when we left Belfast
My teeth like dice were rattlin',
On board a boat unfit for swine
We sailed for Bonnie Scotlan'
But where's the joy in goin' aboard
There's little if there's any
The sea's not all it's bragged to be
Nor Scotland's no sae Bonnie.

We didna see a Highlan' fling
Nor hear the pipers chanter,
They dinna even smoke clay pipes
Nor wear the Tam-o-Shanter.
They're a' sae cool and cannie goin'
You'd hardly see them budging
Altho' the Scots I must admit
Are dacent and obliging.

We saw their buildings great and small
And listened to them boostin'
In fact we saw the world itself
Displayed at Bellahouston.
But not the famous Scotch blue bells
Nor bonnie purple heather
In poetry praised by Rabbie Burns
And sung by Harry Lauder.

But, oh, the things I hated most
I'll bear in mind the longest
Because we thought when comin' home
That Providence had wronged us
The tempest blew from every airt
And caused a tidal splatter
The ship I think did everything
But settle on the water.

A sailor sittin' counting beads
   And sucking at a sausage
Declared that this would likely be
   His final prayer and passage.
For folk were dottering o'er the deck
   Like darkies dancing rumbas,
I'm sure such nights were seldom seen
   By Christopher Columbus.

A Bellamena buddy swore
   He seldom felt unaisy
But listening to this barken batch
   Is goin' to drive me crazy,
"You'd think," says he, "they couldna cough
   They look so mim and swanky
And every time they boke, they bray
   Like Tommy Trimble's donkey."

Thinks I if that's the sail you get
   In just a trip to Glasgo'
Lord help the seasick souls that sail
   As far as San Francisco.
But I'll be older ere I search
   For pleasure o'er the Channel
Unless somebody builds a bridge
   Or drills a blinken tunnel.

The Rolway Lane

I'm just a crazy countryman, frae up amang the hills,
With ne'er a chance to share romance, or love's exciting thrills
It seemed my pals could aye get dolls, but I had never nane
Till out I stole an' took a stroll alang the Rolway Lane.

Beside a style I stops a while, and low it came to pass,
My heart was captivated by a bonnie black-haired lass,
Of course I knew her lang ago, when she was just a wean,
When it used to be the Railway line instead of Rolway Lane.

But noo she's big an' beautifull, her heart is light an' free
She hae's nae fau't or ought like that, except goin' oot wi' me
I know I'm rough an' raw enough, the courtin's coorse an' plain,
Still many a girl enjoys a birl alang the Rolway Lane.

As lang as providence permits, I'll see her yince a week,
To feel her warm arm aroon mi neck, her chin against mi cheek,
Let rain or hail, or storms prevail, she never waits in vain
For I would hate to miss a date alang the Rolway Lane.

A place like this for mortal bliss, nae novel'st could invent,
Like the banks an' briggs, an' cabbage rigs that often we frequent
Withoot her noo, in soul it's true, mi heart would break in twain,
But she canny stay an' leeve her day alang the Rolway Lane.

She'll want a man that's mair refined, an' better dressed than me,
Perhaps some city Romeo wi' lots o' L.S.D.
Then fu'-o'-grief, I'll seek relief amang the hills again
And there lament the nights I spent alang the ROLWAY LANE.

"the Hills and Dells of Antrim

The Hills and Dells of Antrim

There are many sights which claim a part
In everybody's breast
But there's always some place to the heart
More dear than all the rest.
So to me no matter where I roam
There's not a place on earth
Like the Hills and Dells of Antrim
The County of my birth.

With its mystic purple mountains
And winding vales between
Its crystal streams and fountains
And shady groves so green
You would think that Mother Nature
Who fashioned all things fair
In the painting of her picture
Had lingered longer there.

If you ever wander 'oer a brae
Or by a fragrant shade
As the evening sun extends her ray
O'er mountain, glen and glade.
When various hues bedeck the skies
And clothe the countryside
It would mind you of a paradise
Where angels might reside.

And besides that matchless beauty
Tho' fair without a flaw,
It's a land where Love is duty
And Charity is law
Tho' the cottage may be humble
The table poorly spread
There is neither grudge nor grumble
Nor selfishness displayed.

So as long as I be spared to live
Where peace and beauty dwells
Oh, may I never cease to love
My native Hills and Dells
But serve with confidence and pride
My Country and my God
Until my weary bones are laid
Beneath its verdant sod.

"the Ballyeaston Band"

Ballyeaston Band

Of all the music I have heard
   Within my native land
The sweetest tunes were rendered by
   The Ballyeaston Band.

There's no' a band in all the land
   Their equal could supply
For either local picnics or
   The Twelfth Day o' July.

When they begin to play a tune
   It makes your heart feel gay
To hear them pouring forth sweet strains
   Of charming melody.

Should cares and sorrows seize your soul
   Or fate of fun deprive you
I'll swear or bet from such a state
   They've power to revive you.

You listen while those soothing strains
   Their healing charms extend
Yet wondering how those flutes and drums
   Produce a winning blend.

I know their teacher far excels
   The common type o' tutors
And he admits you couldn't find
   A flock o' finer fluters.

But then besides they've something else
   That few flute bands possess
And what that something is I doubt
   If language could express.

If they who first its fashion formed
   Say fifty years ago
Were just allowed to leave the dead
   To hear a tune or two.

They'd be amazed and feel as though
   They stood on holy ground
And doubt if angels up above
   Could make a sweeter sound.

For instance lest you scorn their worth
   Or doubt their reputation
They've took the test with Ulster's Best
   In open competition.

And twice they've been victorious
   O'er bands of high repute
Which proves their great ability
   At tootin' on the flute.

An' feats like these, it's understood
   Can only be achieved
By every member making good
   The talent he received.

So let the thirsty follower that
   Frequents the village pub
Remember them as he conducts
   The goblet to his gub.

An' let the pious also pray
   With elevated hand
The cup of fame may long remain
   With Ballyeaston Band.

Kathleen

Tonight I'm sad and lonely, my heart is sore with pain
Because I know that you and I may never meet again,
We've shared affections, pleasures, and many we have seen,
But gone it seems, my plans and dreams
For you and I, Kathleen.

When we became acquainted, in those happy days gone by
No Irish heart, however blithe, was happier than I.
The wild birds sang so sweetly, the fields were fresh and green
For Nature dressed and wore her best
For you and I, Kathleen.

You were my best companion, my princess and my pride
The only girl in all the worl', I hoped would be my bride.
But somehow fate beguiled us, misforture came between,
And marred the schemes that crowned my dreams
For you and I, Kathleen.

Perhaps I loved too fondly, and soon we will forget,
"Twere better for us both perhaps if we had never met,
Still sometimes I'll be thinking, of just what might have been
If I'd not met Jean, who came between
You and I, Kathleen.

An Irish Emigrant

Sweetheart, tenant of my breast
and joy to my repose
In answer to your kind request
my picture I enclose.

I need no picture as I rove
to keep when we're apart
Because your photo framed with love
Is hanging in my heart.

When I have reached yon heathery hills
beyond the raging blue
Thro' all my many thrills and spills
I'll still remember you.

The Heelan' Jeans an' lowland Megs
may a' sae bonnie be
Wi' tartan skirts and bendy legs
An' buckles on their knee.

But kilty cled nor porridge fed,
Nor face, how ever fair
Can e'er surpass the dacent lass
I leave in Ballyclare.

So do not weep, but ere you sleep
While kneeling by your bunk
Please mention me, a soul at sea,
In case my ship gets sunk.

The Pretty Country Maid

Beyond the green Glenwherry hills
There dwells a pretty maid,
Where the rocky slopes of Slemish meet
The valley of the Braid.
Of all its queens, and gay colleens,
Tho' many and fair they be,
No maid was ere more sweet and rare,
Nor beautiful than she.

She's sweeter than the heather bell,
Or the blossom on the thorn,
And happy as the lark that sings
To greet the early morn.
There's life and laughter in her voice,
It's music when she speaks,
And all the while a cheerful smile
Steals gently o'er her cheeks.

I've watched the shadows cross the glen,
And the sunset o'er the ling,
I've seen the hedges change their hue,
And heard the wild-birds sing,
But never sight however bright,
Nor sound however sweet,
Could joys distil, with the same sweet thrill
As the maid I long to meet.

She yet may leave her native plains,
Or be another's bride,
And I myself find someone else
To grace my fireside.
The glens and glades may change their shades,
And even memories fade,
But I know I'll still remember well,
The PRETTY COUNTRY MAID.

Answer to Leap Year Proposal

Dear Eve: Your challenge or proposal
Is far beyond my pritta – roosel
Why did ye draw your rusty sword
Demanding what I can't afford
Except your will, withholds my name in't
I'll send ye neither cheque nor raiment
Nay, even then I might decline
To clothe a frame that isn'y mine
But anything before I'd wed thee
For faith I cou'dn'y feed nor bed thee
You see, I dinny claim a spot
Except my ain bit lowly cott
And, oh, alas it's rather sma'
It wou'dny houl us baith ava
Besides my brethren or my fether
Might turn us oo't amang the heather
An' on the solitude tha gither
We'd mebby murder yin-an-ither.

Yet if your lonely "Leap Year passion"
Mann find in haste a destination
Just advertise your situation
Wi shouts o' love in desperation
Or mebby fate (whate'er the kine be)
In four years hence, a maid will find ye.

But noo I hope and trust sincerely
You'll no be left ta'e bid Leap-Yearly
Instead I'd like to see ye tied
Wi' bonds that bind a bashful bride
To take a step in that direction
You must be armed wi' fond affection
To share a love like faithfu' mothers
An' no' a pill polluting others.

But here I must conclude my sermon
My text was rude and far frae charmin'
So cheerio; and please excuse me
If by false judgement I accuse ye.

Congratulations

To you and yours these simple lines
   My compliments conveys
To say that may you both be blest
   With many happy days.

May fairest fortune yield her store
   To you and to your wife
With all the blessed thrills and spills
   That come with married life.

'Tis I, who'd like to see you float
   On fortune's wealthy stream
On riches not of land or gold
   But something more supreme.

For mind it's not the heavy purse
   That makes the happy home
Beside 'twould be as bad or worse
   To live by love alone.

But say you had a share of each
   To stock your new estate
What wealth would cancel poverty
   What love could cancel hate.

Then you could make your house a home
   In every kind of weather
And share each others' joys and cares
   While growing old together.

At Eventide

Just by the dusky eventide
As warbling birds retire
My thoughts depart on speedy wing
To the virgin I admire.

I can't forget the happy hours
We fondly wear away
Her picture seems so deep engraved
Upon my memory.

She's one that any lad would love
Or try to woo and win
The kind that none would wish to slight
Nor feel ashamed to own.

Her reputation is complete
No flaw can I discover
The more I think on her, in fact
I find the more I love her.

No paint, nor powder she applies
No sham, no imitation
Her face is o' the bonnie few
That needs no alteration.

It's when she's in amongst a crowd
The odds is plainly shown
She just would mind you o' a rose
Amongst the bramble growin'.

Or like the laurel, evergreen
Whose nature never alters
She keeps in store a thought for me
That never fades, nor falters.

So that's the reason why I think
Each time I see her smile
There's not a colleen half so sweet
In a' the Emerald Isle.

Lorna Doon

There's a garden near Belfast
That I'm sure you've often passed
Where the city people gather blooms in June
But the fairest flower there
Is a girl with flaxen hair
And she's known to the world as "Lorna Doon".

In my eyes she's fairer far
Than Broadway film star
And I'll swear by all that's underneath the moon
If this little Isle o' Green
Were to have a beauty queen
They would put the crown on "Lovely Lorna Doon".

There's a neatness in her style
And a sweetness in her smile
That would charm an Enniskillen Dragoon
And there's no' an Irish lad
But would offer all he had
For the heart and hand of lovely "Lorna Doon".

I've been thinking 'twould be fine
Should she promise to be mine
It's a lump o' luck that couldn't come too soon
In a little bungalow
Where those fragrant flowers grow
I could live forever there with "Lorna Doon".

The Faithful Lover

When death applied the parting stroke
And she was laid to rest
Nobody missed her presence more
Than he who loved her best.

They say in boyhood's sunny days
She set his heart aflame
In manhood's blossoming hour, he
Adored her just the same.

She loved him too, and often vowed
She'd be his very own
Three times she gave consent, and twice
Prepared the bridal gown.

But mystery robs that rare romance
And likely always will
Because they never wed and yet
They loved each other still.

'Twas said he always put it off
By finding something wrong
And many wondered why she kept
So loyal for so long.

But she had sworn to be true
Nor be another's bride
And so her pledge she kept, till she
An aged woman died.

And now she's dead and passed away
No balm however blest
Can soothe the gnawing emptiness
That aches within his breast.

For now he knows there's nothing left
But dreams of days gone by
Memories that fill a broken heart
And fix an absent eye.

A Disappointment

On Thursday night at eight o'clock
Beneath yon willow tree
I understood you had agreed
That with me you would be.

I waited there for half an hour
And patiently did bear
With nothing to encourage me
But silence and despair.

I wondered while I tarried there
Why you had stayed away
A thousand reasons I conceived
Concerning your delay.

In vain I sought for thought that would
Consoling peace impart
For, oh, a load of loneliness
Lay heavy at my heart.

At length I asked myself was I
Worthy of a thought
Or of so little consequence
That probably you'd forgot.

For, oh, the heart is sorely pierced
As with a surgeon's lance
When such occurs to those like me
With no experience.

So to my dwelling I returned
To find the cause explained
The message you had sent had been
Neglected and detained.

So sweet of you informing me
Why you could not attend
Indeed your generous qualities
I highly recommend.

In fact I felt that I'd been loved
Instead of disappointed
Not only by the note you sent
But the reason you had sent it.

Oh stupid youth, how oft the foe
   That cripples thy devotion
When scrutinized by proper sense
   Is just a foolish notion.

It seems as such has been the case
   In this my short romance
An' honestly I feel ashamed
   To ask another chance.

So fling this fruitless flame aside
   As if it hadn't been
And I shall try to pass it by
   As if it were a dream.

In Loneliness

At night when songsters cease to sing
Amongst the fragrant bowers
And weary silence reigns throughout
The long and lonesome hours.

It's then I think on her I love
And long to have her near me
For just the lingering memories
Are all I have to cheer me.

She's all that's near and dear to me
In short, she's all I care for
I know of none so sweet and fair
To whom I might compare her.

Should someone else come in between
And gain her fond affection
I think to be deprived of her
Would drive me to distraction.

Tho' friendship ties have often broke
And lovers oft' have parted
The victims of the parting stroke
Are seldom brokenhearted.

Yet I at present couldn't bear
A moment's separation
For she, of all my heart and soul
Has absolute possession.

So for an ardent wooer's sake
Ye angels up above her
Be pleased to visit her in dreams
And tell her that "I love her."

And Thou who guides the virtuous fair,
From every foe defend her
And where she is be also there
That goodness may attend her.

A Scholar's Lament

Dear Teacher, just a moment take
And read this rhyme just for my sake
It may not be a first class make
  Still I've no better
'Twill give your interests a shake
  This blasted letter.

Oh, hard's the task to teach and train
A thick numbskull, minus the brain
Could you his mind a moment gain
  You'd make him clever
Or carve a spot, which would remain
  On him forever.

The senseless youngsters roaring wild
It's hard to make them meek and mild
The question's first can bones be filed
  And changed to brain
Spare not the rod to spoil the child
  Use you the cane.

When young, if then we don't begin
To know the righteous acts from sin
There's none could put new wisdom in
  To vanish scorn
It must be there engraved within
  Before we're born.

We used to stand and stare and stammer
An' try to parse a phrase o' grammar
Oh how the map we used to hammer
  And make it shiver
Or peer and scorch and claw and clammer
  For town and river.

Oh, in the school we often thought
Life was the hardest battle fought
What made things worse was when you caught
  Me by the collar
Although the method which you taught
  Made me a scholar.

I thought there whiles that you were tough
At times I got it kind o' rough
'Twas then that I beheld a brough
  Round stars and moon
But still I did not get enough
  Nor yet too soon.

I'm sure you're glad to give up teaching
And for a tempting pension reaching
Far from the din a children screeching
  And threatening mothers
For always of some ill they're preaching
  Of yours or others.

Whenever you quit this human race
And start the golden path to pace
Please take the "Roll Book" to that place
  If it would fit us.
And call aloud our names in grace
  Lest they forget us.

Divide the glory free for all
Substract all ill from great and small
And multiply in case we fall
  Our gracious deeds
And in addition to this call
  Provide our needs.

To speak the truth, and speak my mind
To us you were both good and kind
And may you consolation find
  For what you've wrought
Accept this rhyme though roughly lined
  From one you taught.

"A Battle with Buttons"

A Battle with Buttons

The ither night 'way efter nine
The day an' date I daeny mine
Our folks were a' tae bed, bar three
The boss, ye see, an' Jack an' me.
When three the "Master" fu' o' fight
Steps in to spend a happy night
You know the "Masters" checker mad
An' oor oul' lad, he's just as bad
They didny sit a tie thegether
Until they challenged yin an' ither
The baerd was brought wi' muckle haste
An' soon they had the buttons placed
When each had cracked his usual joke
'Twas then decided they would smoke
My fether han's me oot his cutty
Commandin' me to dae my duty
Wi' that Jack taps me on the shouther
An' whispers "Plug the pipe wi' pouther"
'Course I agreed wi' his suggestion
An' soon the scheme was put in action.

When pipes were placed in snug position
The meek curled up in homely fashion
Then startin' off wi' fresher fettle
To end that silent, sight sure battle
Each eyed the other's situation.
As if 'twas "Nation versus Nation"
The fight was tight, an' aught but speedy
For baith were feared, an' cute and greedy
The yin was wonderin' very painfu'
How he might move to life a handfu'.
The other planning as he stared
To gie a man an' clean the baerd
But Jack an' me no doubt were restless
For checkers didn't interest us
The seconds passed like weeks o' penance
The clock was a' that broke the silence
But still we braved the sore suspense
Tae see an' hear the consequence.

At length Jack sings it's no' for workin'
When "Bang" the show went jumpin', spankin'
Just a' at yince wi' cracks and flashes.
A shoor o' sparks an' oaths an' ashes
Wheezed here an' there, like splints o' flint.
While baith were burnt, an' nearly blint.

But Jack bi this was up the stairs
A laughin' off his evening prayers
Suppose frae sic a situation
He thought that flight would be salvation
Yet I tae stem a future ruction
Confessed it was a dirty action
"But mine," says I, 'twas just for sportie
"We tried to scare, but no tae hurt ye
Yous luk like twa distracted folk
It's queer ye's cannie see the joke."
"What, see the joke?" they yelled the 'gither
Sure yin can scarcely see the ither
And where's the fun that could be seen o't
In trying tae blaw a buddy's ee'n o'ot."

However when the tempest ceased
An' peace throughout the calm increased
The pipes once more were got agoin'
(This time each filled an' lit his own)
So when I saw the fun had flitted
I went tae bed an' left them at it.

The Mester

I have heard people brag about places they've been
How far they have travelled, the sights they have seen;
But the happiest memories of most, as a rule,
Are the days of their childhood they spent at the school.
With me it was different; when I was a boy
The school had no pleasure, no spasms of joy.
I was'ny content from the first day I went
For I would'ny been there if I had'ny been sent.
Nor I was'ny lucky as ithers I know
Who got sweeties and pennies to coax them to go;
For money was scanty and leather was dear;
I went in my bare yins three months of the year.

I was'ny long started before I could tell
That very few present knew less than mysel';
I had great difficulty dividing by two
If the figure was bigger I had'ny a clue.
Forbye I discovered how far I was wrang
About things I was sure I was right for so lang.
I could see that Creation – from what I was taught –
Was more of a mystery than even I thought;
For instance, the Earth has no corners at all
For the World is a planet the shape of a ball
Surrounded by galaxies spinnin' in space
With apparently nothing to keep it in place.

And away beyond Ireland there's people galore
In places I never heard mentioned before;
With cultures so varied, and countries so vast
They have cities far bigger than Larne or Belfast.

The scholars by nature were shuffled apart
Some lazy and stupid, some quick and alert.
Some acted like infants long into their teens
While ithers had minds like computer machines.
To queries and theories I played little heed
My future depended on learnin' a trade.
So I sat thro' the sessions of borin' details
Just suckin' my pencil or bitin' my nails.
If the teacher approached me I made some excuse
Or ask for permission to use the wee hoose.

Now the Mester's a man of unquestionable skill
And determined that nothing would alter his will
To ensure that the parents took pride in their wee'ns
While he was in charge of their bodies and brains.
Their morals and manners as much his concern
As the edification they ventured to learn.
His methods were simple, the standard was high
And God help the pupil that did'ny comply.

When he asked you a question on what you had read
Or to prove you'd been listening to what he had said
It was'ny so bad wi' a minute to think
But if asked in a hurry, the mind would go blank.
The answers were seldom, if ever, correct,
And as often an answer he did'ny expect.
Sometimes he would gulder, sometimes he would grin
A lot would depend on the mood he was in.

When a comic committed some minor offence
Like playing a prank at the Mester's expense,
He'd punish some innocent creat're like me,
And the guilty but cunning wee rascal went free.
When I think on the wallops I got wi' the cane
The taps o' my fingers still dinnel wi' pain.
I min' at the time how I felt I would like
Just to hide a wee bomb in the bag o' my byke.
For convinced that revenge was a bit of a risk
In case I got jammed between him and the desk.
I decided to wait till my muscles matured
Or else get my heed and my shoulders insured.

And woe to the villain that kicked a wee lass
Or was rude to the teacher in front of the class.
If the cane was'ny handy to gie' him a scud
He just took his knuckles and thumped him a thud.

Sometimes I look back at those delicate years
My chums now secure in their jobs and careers.
And I wonder how many would care to confess
That they owe to the Mester their wealth and success.
Some teachers, some preachers and pillars of peace,
Some doctors, some lawyers, a few on the police.
And as many have seen their ambition fulfilled
By the wisdom and knowledge his teaching instilled.

As for me, when I think on the blunders I made
No wonder the threads of his patience got frayed,
And yet, he was kind, to a certain degree
Altho' there was friction between him and me.

Since then he's retired, our feud's at an end
I'm honoured and proud when he calls me his friend.
And now when I meet him he just shakes my han'
Which proves he's a generous, agreeable man.

The Duke of Windsor

Here was a Prince who was much beloved
The sweetest that ever lived and moved
A "Prince" who was welcome any place
Loved and honoured by every race.
People awaited the happy hour
When he would be crowned King Emperor
Statesmen drank to their future King
And the prosperous years that his reign would bring
Members of Parliament pledged their word
While loyal subjects felt assured
That he would be King of the truest kind
And reign as never King had reigned.

But, alas, as the appointed hour drew nigh
And every loyal heart beat high
He denounced every title he possessed
For the beautiful lady he loved the best.
A lady, as far as we understand
Unfit to be Queen of England
Because she was married twice and of course
From each of her husbands won divorce.
It didn't look well to the average eye
To see her ascend to the Monarchy
Therefore the King for his future chose
The presence of her whom he dare not lose.
For without her sweet words, her fond embrace
His reign would be void of happiness.

Some were amazed at what he'd done
Some had pity, others none
Clergymen were the most dismayed
At the strange decision he had made.
"Strange," they said, I suppose because
'Twas contrary to Bible and British laws.

But why do they utter a harsh rebuke
And spitefully chasten the banished Duke?
If he has fallen and "Love" the cause
It's a natural failing that always was
That men will exchange all the wealth they have
For that something more precious than wealth can give.

Such was the lot of the first of men
To him, without Eve, sure his life was vain
"King" of all creatures, of every birth
"King" of a beautiful new-born earth.
All that was pleasant, pure and fair
Everything good was surely there.
There in that realm, he knew and felt
His was where peace and plenty dwelt
Yet there was something he still required
Something his heart of hearts desired.
Where was the pleasure it all supplied
When none but himself its joy enjoyed
"Could no one," he wondered, "be with him there"
That they might of his power and glory share.

So while that passion stirred his breast
The lonely Monarch would not rest
Till the great creator we believe
Gave him a partner, the woman Eve.

And Samson the strongest that ever was
Both reared and taught by the strictest laws
Did not he cling to the Philistine
A damsel alien to his kith and kin.
And why? because 'twas her he loved
As he later his trust and affection proved
When he told her a secret he would not tell
For hope of Heaven, or fear of Hell
And even "David" the Psalmist King
Who was blest with almost everything
He stained the repute of his virtuous life
By falling in love with his servant's wife.
People were stunned by the strange romance
Captains would hinder at every chance
But the King in his heart was not satisfied
Until he had won his unlawful bride.
And he went as far to achieve that aim
As having her husband Uriah slain.

So – grave as the situation seems
And much as the King's abdication means
If we think on the burdens Kings must bear
Within such a closely guarded sphere.
We would not blame the charming Duke
For the choice he made, nor the step he took
But wish him success where 'ere he be
With her he loves so faithfully.

The Three Brave Men

'Twas on a night both dark and drear, near pritta diggin' time o' year
As three o' the bravest men in Erin were sittin' by the wayside yarnin,
When suddenly they heard a howl, the kine that makes yer blood rin cowl,
'Twas like an animal distracted – or by some fearfu' pain attacked.

The noise had scarcely took the wines, when half a dozen number nines
Were peltin' off in hot pursuit to seek and save that helpless brute.
Through hedge and ditch they madly tear, as if there had been naething there
For naught it seemed in time o' need could stem their strength or mar their speed.

Swift as the wind they onward spank until they reach the river's bank,
Here Jack went down and Billie trippet, but Batter skimmed it like a whippet,
Nae, less his flight is cancelled there, he hangs a second in the air,
Caught by the pants or something mair, on brand new galvanised barbed wire.

A struggle then a painful yelp, a rip, then Batter cries for help.
"Where are ye, boys, come quick," he said, "My case requires instant aid"
"I'm here," cries Jack. "A helpless wreck, wi' Billy's heels aroon my neck,
Besides what makes it less supreme, I'm lying prostrate in the stream."

"Then how the . . . could I assist, and me about to breathe my last,
A minute more in such a state, my soul and flesh must separate,
And never did it strike my faith that I should die a double daith,
The very thought it makes me wince, tae be baith hanged and drooned at yince.

But Batter "min' if you survive – for some cruel reason you're kept alive,
Go warn the friends that I've forsaken, lest they be took as I've been taken"
But Batter didnay heed his pleas, instead he clamoured for release,
An' aye frae toward the suffering beast, the howls of agony increased.

At last through wrath an' pain an' fear, the strain was more than they could bear,
'Twas then alas a battle brewed, a war of evil words ensued
The atmosphere wi' terror blazed, as each his feelings freely phrased,
There Jack was swearing he was hung, while Batter spoke an unknown tongue.

An' Billie (though 'twas sore duration) was trying to restore his patience,
But slowly Billie starts tae swear, and poured it forth so like a prayer
That Jack forgot his present state, an' reverently took off his cap,
Indeed the scene was bad but brief, so fierce in fact, it's my belief
Had Nick himself come on the scene, he would hae been scared to intervene.

At length they got their bosoms eased, and from their bondage were released,
And very soon resumed their search, which didna' take them fifty perch,
Till lo behold they found her there – the cow that caused the whole affair,
There on the ground she lay and quivered, in hope that she might be delivered.

Now here's where I came interfering, I also heard what they'd been hearing,
Then started through the fields assaunterin', an' gallivantin' wi' a lantern,
I hadn'y reached the place, so far, till there a voice cries "What's wrang there"
Says I "I'm lookin' for a coo that I heard growlin' like a soo."

"Come here," they said, "And don't be skio" so I approached the panting trio
And though the lamp was dim and sooty, they soon performed the nee'ful duty
Well, man, the job was scarce complete, till up she staggers tae her feet
An' off she goes just wi' a yell, a dashing through the dark like . . . well.

You see she saw the crowd around her, so why she went there's little wonder
Once more in strains both rough and strong, she emphasised her woefu' song
For miles around baith lang and hoarse, the cattle joined in roaring chorus
In faith I thought – I don't know why, the end o' time was drawing nigh.
An' still a thing that often happens, I just was bate to keep from laughin,
So I began to gae and giggle, but soon the heros gien a baggle
They stared as if prepared to murder, then asked a question like an order
"What makes ye laugh in time o' sorrow?, be aff an' fetch a blinkin' borrow
That we may wheel the slink tae shelter, before the thing goes helter skelter."

It's you, I'll be glad tae tell the news; twill suit your personal private views
Now houl your tongue, it doesna' matter, but you adore the neighbour's daughter
Well off I went without a word, an' soon had reached the neighbour's yard,
Just when I rapped I heard a din that told me there was life within
As Maggie staggers out o' bed, an' through the window thrust her head.

"Who's that?" she cries, "at sich an 'oor?" "It's me," says I, "That's at your door"
An' ere she got the door right appaned I hastily explained what happened.
When Maggie heard my gruesome story. she got in a desperate flurry,
An' ordered Madge tae get her skit on (the yin that I was blamed for courtin').

So when they got themselves prepared, we got the borrow an' left the yard,
An' made our way o'er moor an' fen, to find once more the three brave men,
Who with their jokes had soon begun a bit o' rough an' ready fun
Indeed sae jolly was the crew, we were homeward bound before we knew.

An' even when we had arrived, the merriment and laughter thrived,
Says I with what I've heard and seen, I've watched worse sketches on the screen
Had I the films phonie fixtures an' things for taking talkie pictures,
I could hae got the Graphic fellow a chapter for his "Western thriller".

"But come, we'll make for home," I said "An' let the folks get back to bed
For yarns like these are only vain, we'll talk it o'er some time again."
So finally we left the yard, as Maggie spoke a farewell word
"You'll make a poem on this," she said, "I will," says I – an' so I did.

Bonnie Gertie

In search o'joys we oft pursue
The sex that wear the skirtie
Tho' some are rude
An' boul and pro'd
An' ithers din and dirty.

But no such faults are found with her
The one I used tae courtie
She's clean an' neat
An a' thats sweet
I call her bonnie Gertie.

No matter how the win would blow
Wi her I aye felt heartie
'Twas my delight
On a winter night
To see her faya Party.

But once I saw her wi the Yank
Thats lately frae Alberta
They looked so fit,
Thinks I see yet
Your gettin rather sportie.

So I fulfilled my final tryst.
And told her she was flirty
So ended once
A short romance
With me an' bonnie Gertie.

Mollie and the Ghost

The lightning flashed, the thunder roared
  The rain in torrents fell
On such a dreadful night occurred
  The tale I have to tell.
Benighted was an ancient dame
  And much against her will
She had to come from "Killylane"
  Through "Jonnie Gilmour's Hill".

Well, this the path that she pursued
  Would cross a haunted bridge
Where ghosts and fairies parleyvoo'd
  About the river edge.
Where witches, when the sun has set
  Have games of choose and chase
And where 'twas said a doctor met
  The devil face to face.

As Mollie battled o'er the braes
  Against the drenching rain
The ghastly deeds of bygone days
  Came flashing o'er her brain.
But oft she consolation sought
  As to herself she said
It's only those of sinful thought
  Have cause to be afraid.

So as she neared the haunted bridge
  She thought she heard a squeal
When something from the hawthorn hedge
  Came trotting past her heel.
She stopped and listened, stiff and scared
  To hear what made her start
To her relief she only heard
  The pounding of her heart.

But as she started on her prowl
  She heard it cry again
'Twas like a poor departed soul
  In Purgatorial pain.
As terror seized her quaking frame
  Her faith she could not boast
Nor would she search from whence it came
  In case it was a ghost.

So feared, lest this might be her doom
From thence she must make haste
When dimly through the cheating gloom
She spied an awful beast.
Like captured by its blackest art
She screamed and held her breast
And rapidly within her heart
She many sins confessed.

Then up the lonely lane she fled
And over "Grannies Forth"
Along the county road she sped
For what her legs were worth.
Though all her pep and patience lost
Her pace she dare not slack
For much she feared the grizzling ghost
Would seize her by the neck.

To home, tho' fearful haste she made
It seemed an awful length
A second time she knelt and prayed
For God to give her strength
For knowing well its wicked cause
It horrified her brain
To hear the patter of its paws
And clanging of its chain.

At last she reached her "butt and ben"
Wherein her safety lay
Resolving should she stray again
To come some other way.
And with a heavy wooden leg
She quickly propped the door
While by her side her faithful dog
Lay panting on the floor.

He like a kindly canine pal
Had broken from his post
And followed her, so ends the tale
Of "Mollie and the Ghost".
So that was how the people say
The "Black-bridge" got its name
And other haunted places may
Perhaps be just the same.

A Drunkard

Here's the story of a student
Going forth to make a claim
To be with the wise and prudent
Was his ever earnest aim.

To become a leading lawyer
To be truthful, quick and strong
Executing peace and justice
O'er the scale of right and wrong.

Well equipped with education
Making good his flight to fame
While distant friends became relations
To his seeming prosperous name.

To the summit he was marching
Blind with confidence and pride
Little knowing foul misfortune
Lurked behind the other side.

When he reached his destination
Crowned with honour and success
He had gained a situation
Just the cleverist could possess.

Soon his pleas were so commanding
And his reason was so wise
That e'en the great in understanding
Sought his counsel and advice.

Seldom were his plans rejected
Men admired the deeds he'd done
Both the rich and poor respected
The reputation he had won.

Life from him withheld no treasure
He had all that he required
Entertainment, wealth and pleasure
Fed and clad as he desired.

Oft of goblets overflowing
He was tempted to partake
Sometimes he would quaff the contents
For his kind companions' sake.

Oft he drank in social fashion
Yet he saw no danger there
But alas that cursed temptation
Dragged him slowly to despair.

Soon his heart was cut and cankered.
To an awful craving state
And finally he became a drunkard
Staggering on the verge of fate.

Eventually with many trials
Resting on his tortured brain
All his chief supporting morals
Broke beneath the constant strain.

Then ashamed and brokenhearted
To the bottom he was cast
Lower still than where he started
In the not far distant past.

Very few take pity.on him
People loathe his presence nigh
Pals and friends alike disown him
Distant strangers pass him by.

Once a rich, distinguished figure
At the highest peak of fame
Now a hopeless, helpless beggar
Doomed to poverty and shame.

Such has been the short career
Of a person we know well
And perhaps there's many others
Who have likewise rose and fell.

"Saint Patrick"

As soon as Slemish comes in view, 'tho far away and faint
It brings to mind the life and times of Ireland's Patron Saint.
'Twas there he spent his early teens, attending sheep and swine,
According to the history books in days of "Auld Lang Syne".
The boy was brought from Bristol by rogues who used to steal
For Nial an oul ancestor of the present Lord O'Neill.
He worked awhile for Oul King Nial near Tara's famous hall
But this was long before the harp was hung on Tara's wall.
Then Pat was sold – a slave we're told – and forcibly was made
To serve a noble named Milchu, a pagan from the Braid.
This wealthy County Antrim man was chieftain o' a Clan
And lord of great possessions from the Battery to the Bann.
He lacked for nothing gold could buy, and ruled with heavy hand,
Had men and maids with skills and trades to jump at his command.
With ample serfs to win' his turn and tend his barley rigs,
Wee Paddy, like the Prodigal, was lumbered with the pigs.

Up on the mountain, wild and bare, while trampin' round the herd
He little thought his destiny, it's reason and reward.
That these the barren rocks he trod in bleak obscurity
Would be a shrine of pilgrimage left for posterity.
Sometimes to ease his naked feet he'd sit down on a stone
And gaze across the countryside towards Derry and Tyrone.
The moors and fens, the woods and glens, so peaceful and serene
Spread like a carpet interspersed with every shade of green.
'Tho his heart was with his kinfolk in the country of his birth
He knew his eyes would never see a fairer place on earth.

To pass the time in winter, when the hills were white with snow
He'd mingle with the peasants in the valley down below.
To learn their language and their laws, their rituals and their feuds
The powers and the duties of the Brehons and the Druids.
He found to help a stranger they were naturally inclined
'Tho mostly poor and ignorant they were friendly and kind.
The native Celts wore brogues and pelts and worshipped pagan gods,
And dwelt in caves and cromlechs, or hovels built with sods.
To pacify the bogeyman some babes were burned at stakes
And wee thorn threes were shelters for the fairies from the snakes.
Oft' Pat petitioned Providence to save the simple race
And bring a bit o' gumption to the god-forgotten place.
The hope that one day he'd be free would often cross his mind
To leave the bonds of slavery and the Slemish hills behind.
Away from ruthless raiders like the Spaniard and the Dane
And hordes of plunderin' heathens from Glenwherry and Broughshane.

A plan took shape for Pat's escape and when he got the chance
He sailed away from Carnlough Bay and ended up in France.
Convinced that God had called him to attend to greater things
He'd spend his days in search of ways to serve the King of Kings.
He studied rolls of ancient scrolls preserved in holy shrines,
Recorded there by witnesses in early Bible times.
And so from books and testaments the knowledge he obtained
He qualified for service and as bishop was ordained.

One day to Saul in County Down a preacher he returned
By God's permission to expound the Scripture he had learned.
He notified the local chief to congregate his clan
To hear the words in Genesis concerning God and man.
The reason Adam's race was doomed to sorrow, toil and strife
And robbed of their inheritance to everlasting life.
Of generations long deceased who wandered round like sheep,
And entered into covenants that few were fit to keep.
But God, because He loved the world, has sent His only Son
To take their place and pay for all the evil they have done.
He then explained the Virgin birth and how it came to pass;
The life and works of Jesus from the manger to the Cross.
And how the Jews and Romans jeered and said he was a fraud
Until his resurrection proved he was the Son of God.
The pagan chief with great relief began to comprehend
That life was more than meat and drink, and death was not the end.
He turned his barn into a church where Pat could preach awhile,
The first of many to be built throughout the Emerald Isle.
Like fire the Gospel message spread to every hill and glen,
And this became a Land of Saints and educated men.

It's fifteen hundred years since then, the Kingdom nearer hand;
We worship still our capital, our cattle and our land.
Then what has Patrick's mission been – a blessing or a curse?
Without the Slemish slave or saint would Ireland be worse?
The christian view now split in two, the Papist and the Prod.
Do we behave like children in the family of God?
It seems we're tethered to a tribe and much the same as then
Religion still means politics to fighting Irish men.

Wee Jamie Porter

Wee Jamie Porter lived alone, and happy he abode
In an old converted army hut, beside the Braepark road,
He led a simple life, for often unemployed
He lacked the love and luxury most workin' men enjoyed.

His friends were few and most he knew -- his company ignored,
Except when he could give them gifts that he could ill afford,
But what he spent, or where it went, he never seemed concerned,
Thro' kindness or thro' carelessness, he squandered all he earned.

Sometimes he took a drap o'drink, and when he took too much
His brain with other faculties got badly out of touch,
For alcohol among the blood upsets the natural plan
And often unintentionally presents a different man.

But Jamie was a quiet man, and seldom went astray,
The backward type who thinks a lot, but haven't much to say
He kept his business to himself, and gave offence to none
And truth and honesty prevailed in all he said and done.

But now, alas, he's dead and gone, and nobody seems to care,
His little house is much the same, except there's no one there,
Sometimes I dander down the road, and stop beside the gate,
And think how sad that one so meek should merit such a fate.

My Mother

Of all the friends I e'er possessed
I truly love my mother best,
The one whose love for me shall last
When lighter passions long have passed.

The one whose love has longer dwelt,
More firmly fixed, more keenly felt
Than any touch from Cupid's dart
That for a moment warmed my heart.
And in return I know she knows
While thro' my veins her life blood flows
I love her likewise real and true
Respecting her in all I do.

'Twas her who loved me first and best
Ere I to wooing words could list'.
My infant form she oft caressed
And fondly to her bosom pressed.

My feeble footsteps she would guide,
And gladly for my needs provide.
'Twas her whose soothing words availed
When all attempts but hers had failed,
The one who would from wrong correct me,
And still from hurt or harm protect me.

For all her kindness, all her care,
For all the throes I made her bear
Could I repay the debt I owe her?
Or in return such kindness show her?
Nay, when my best I have committed
I'm still to her as deeply indebted.

But, oh, the thought that grieves me most
Is in the pleasures I have lost,
To say things sweeter than I said
And do things better than I did.
Oft I would scorn her dear advice
And her sweet, chastening words despise,
For I was cruel and unkind
And to her fond affection blind.

But now I see thro' bitter tears
The error of my boyhood years,
Sometimes I think (though thought in vain)
If I could live my life again
What greater patience I would take
To be obedient for her sake,
Her bosom might be less distressed
And more acquaint with happiness.

But now that such a chance has gone
And time is slowly slipping on,
May I be spared to live and move
Till I my true affection prove,
That I through her remaining days
May soothe and comfort her always,
And never once her need neglect,
But aye on her, her love reflect,
Then I shall feel when she is gone
'Twas just my duty I had done.

The Mountain Terrace

Ye look forlorn
An' badly worn
Thou Yett-Brae Mountain Terrace
Since is the cry
You're jilted by
Your previous tenant "Ferris".

Why did ye rise
Wi' tearless eyes?
An' leave this place deserted
Noo a' the folk
That drink and smoke
Are sorely brokenhearted.

A memory brings
Me back to things
That were so often handed
The "Narry Cuts"
An' "Woodbine butts"
Are no' sae much demanded.

Ye would 'tis sure
Ha'e helped the poor
On yin's that had nae sense
Or stood a trate
Wi' any mate
But – at his own expense.

Ye had a score
A thousand more
Of foes, ye had as many
Of friends ye'd less
An' if they'd confess
I think ye hadn'y any.

E'en where y'er noo
Baith hett an' fu
'Mang folk who labour good
If you tak' up
The "Lugless Cup"
Lord help their neigbourhood.

But lissen, sir
Although ye err
You're no' a greed pursuer
There's yin here yet
For hell just fit
An' just as bad as you were.

If that thing death
Would stap your breath
'Twould be nae great disaster
When you go down
Just pinch a crown
An' help your thoughtful master.

'Mang Satan's braves
Murderers an' knaves
You'll fizz like belly bacon
I am and always
Hope to stay
Sincerely, Yours Forsaken.

"Jamies Houdan Hen"

The Highway Code, the Sawmill Road and Jamie's Houdan Hen

There's lights and signs and long white lines, at crossin's, braes and bends
To chart the path where sudden death occasionally descends,
And yet there's fools who spurn the rules – like dames and drunken men,
But the curse that's worst to safety first is Jamie's Houdan hen.

She'll give her rough oul muff a cuff and strut across the road
With no respect, in fact, for acts, much less the Highway Code.
You brake, you swerve, you lose your nerve and nine times oot o' ten
You'll shear a gear bi' steerin' clear o' Jamie's Houdan hen.

She jumps and haps through gaps and slaps, tae fill you fu' o' fear,
The rips and squeals o' brake and wheels is music tae her ear,
There's no' a source, a cause or force ootside the Devil's den
That scrapes or skins mair knees and shins than Jamie's Houdan hen.

She seldom feeds on fleas and seeds, or luks for pritta moul',
Tae hump and kick and claw and pick, like ony ither fowl,
Instead she sits and dabs her hips, tae something comes – and then –
A desperate dash, another crash for Jamie's Houdan hen.

A Pharisee from Ball'nashee was passing on his bike
An' goin' at speed – she knocked him head and shouthers thro' a dyke
Now left with scars where handlebars had gored his abdomen
He blames the code, Sawmill Road, and Jamie's Houdan hen.

I hae run o'er ducks and cats and pups – fell aff an' tore mi coat
An' lost mi share o' skin an' hair, collidin' wi' a goat,
I've kicked the lugs o' biting dugs, frae Kells tae Killyglen,
But I never met a terror yet like Jamie's Houdan hen.

There's folk in splints, wi' limps and squints, a sorry sight to see
An' some got thumps that gien them lumps where hollows used to be,
Tho' blid's been spilt there's nane been kil't, but Heaven knows just when
Your journey's end could yet depend on Jamie's Houdan hen.

The King George V

The world was seized by sorrow's power
And many tears were shed
When in the lonesome midnight hour
We heard the King was dead.

'Tis true that o'er the lowly cot
Such grief and sadness falls
And likewise death its victims find
Within the Palace walls.

So loyal hearts are for a time
On seas of sorrow tossed
While states and nations mourn the fate
Of whom they honoured most.

We knew him not as one of might
Who soars on lofty wing
But as our faithful Governor
As father, friend and King.

His kindly deeds, and soothing words
His people's trust procured
And every colour, creed and tongue
His love and law adored.

Throughout his reign, he always prayed
For universal peace
That every good and glorious cause
Might prosper and increase.

But, oh, alas his constant task
Was one that none could share
And oft the weight of wordly woe
Was more than he could bear.

So now that death has set him free
No more he feels distressed
And with the Almighty King of Kings
We wish his soul at rest.

The Ulster L.D.V.

The last Brigade of British troops
   Were trying to embark
As Nazi Huns with bombs and guns
   Were smashing up Dunkirk.
What saved us then we'll never ken
   Perhaps it was the sea
But well I mind the day I joined
   THE ULSTER L.D.V.

When Churchill saw no help nor hope
   But sweat and toil and tears
The King sent an S.O.S.
   And asked for Volunteers
Up rose recruits in groups of troops
   To set the country free
And the League of Nations christened them
   THE ULSTER L.D.V.

They came from every walk of life
   To save their native land
And soon the news had reached the Reich
   The German High Command.
At once like chaff, the Chiefs of Staff
   Began to flit and flee
Glad to retreat before they'd meet
   THE ULSTER L.D.V.

The Fuhrur feared his fate was sealed
   And tried to take his life,
His generals left the battlefield
   To stem internal strife
Their war machine, their new regime
   Was going all agee
For lack of tact to counteract
   THE ULSTER L.D.V

But Goebbels swore the Fatherland
   Must bring its foes to heel
And prove the Huns were still the sons
   Of concrete, blood and steel
We'll beat the Yanks, the Czechs and Chinks
   And bye and bye, said he
We'll fill the concentration camps
   WITH THE ULSTER L.D.V.

A spurt was put on new designs
Of weapons and machines
The sky was filled with flying bombs,
The sea with submarines
The River Rhine, the Seigfried Line
Would be no guarantee,
So they spared no cash, nor flesh to smash
THE ULSTER L.D.V.

But brawn and brain were spent in vain
As this at length revealed
For after years of blood and tears
The Hun was forced to yield
Then colours, creeds, all tongues and breeds
Prepared a Jubilee
To cheer the brave undaunted slave
THE ULSTER L.D.V.

So when history brags of gallant hearts
Who braved the shot and shell
And monuments proclaim the names
Of those who fought and fell
Remember the scream of the old siren
And the homeless refugee
And the ones who won the war for fun
THE ULSTER L.D.V.

The Crisis

If governments have gold to spend
Is this their wisest plan
Inventing evil implements
To slay their fellowman
Would not the countries' scanty wealth
More happiness secure
Providing food and raiment for
The desolate and the poor.

Will England urge her troops to march
Through Flanders' fateful glen
A field that's strewn with blood and bones
Of Britain's bravest men.
Where tens of thousands fought and bled
Her freedom to obtain
But, oh, I fear if such their view
They must have died in vain.

Or shall we leave our native land
And those we love so well
To dare once more those dreadful deeds
Thro' showers of shot and shell.
While yet a war surviving few
Are crawling on through life
Presenting crippled evidence
Of universal strife.

'Tis everybody's chief desire
Hostilities should cease
But can our noble statesmen find
A path that leads to peace?
While we, the slaves of debt and dread
And threatening woes of war
Are bound and sworn to guard and shield
The heathen from afar.

Should "bold Britannia" need a hand
Against some spiteful foe
'Tis I who'd gladly draw a sword
To lay the aggressor low
But to defend those foreign fiends
Who care not where we sleep
I'll neither toil o'er torrid plains
Nor plough the ocean deep.

So nations that desire to sail
In search of love and peace
May all their ships resist the gale
O'er fortune's surging seas
And may the "Royal Prince of Peace"
Be standing on the shore
To make the troubled seas subside
And their lost hope restore.

Peace in Ballyclare

This wee while back the Worl' has reached a terrible wicked state
Even to die a natural death will soon be out of date.
Wi' murder, suicide and war, and slaughter here and there
The only place there's safety now is here in Ballyclare.

Since armistice was signed and sealed, there's neither peace nor rest
There's either trouble in the East, or terror in the West.
In every corner of the earth there's danger and despair
There's consternation everywhere, except in Ballyclare.

There's how-di-doo in Timbuktoo, there's civil war in Spain,
The Abyssinians want to fight with Italy again,
The Jews and Arabs clash and kill, but dang the hair we care
When Palestine's so many miles away from Ballyclare.

The British try to separate the Germans from the Czechs,
The Russians try to keep the Chinks and Japs on ithers' necks,
And De Valera wants the North, but he has got his share,
He may get ither toons for Eire, but niver Ballyclare.

We want no war, no party strife, no needless expense,
We niver want to split a skull, except in self defence,
We only want what does ourselves, and get it fair and square
And keep all fighting foreigners away from Ballyclare.

Oul Age

I seldom go t' dances noo – I'm gettin o'er oul,
Forbye a hate t' stay oot late – A canny stan' the coul,
Mi legs are no' as soople for mi joints are stiff an' dry
'Am bate ta swing the Hielan' Fling, nae matter ho' a try.

Oul tunes a hear delight my ear – the music sounds sae sweet,
A want tae dance – but canny get the message tae ma feet,
But long ago it was nae so, when I was at my peak
Before I met the wife I went tae two or three a week.

We either rode a bike or walked, to Bl'easton or Tildarg
But places like Glenarm or Larne – we hired Matt Meharg.
An' many a happy night a had, a dancin' roon the floor
Nae odds a lang a dance would last, a always wanted more.
We done the Lancers an' the Setts, the Polka an' the Reels
"Twas great tae hear the tapping feet, and rattling o' the heels
Some watch them glide from side to side as round the floor the' came
While others dance to get the chance to see their partner hame.

The young yins say that's past and gone, we live in a different age
The country dance is oot o' date – the Disco's all the rage
I know they're cute withoot goin' oot – it's on TV at hame
Who knows – in fifty years from noo – they'll say the very same.

"Hard times"

Hard Times

The goat's been dry since last July, the turkey's suckin' eggs
If times get any worse than this, I'll ha' to stap the fags,
To get the cash for chicken mash, I had to sell the sow,
Now I'll hae tae sell the donkey – to buy another cow.

The dungarees that hide my knees are torn round the feet
And thro' the rips aroon my hips – I lose a lot o' heat
Wi' risin' stanes and makin' drains, my back's got out o' shape
To scatter dung when I was young, you only had a graip.

I wonder why so many lang to buy a bit o' lan'
God help you, lad, you must be mad, or away wi' the ban'.
Take my advice, if you be wise, an' get anither job
There's been folk farmin' all their days, and niver made a bob.

To Robert

Youngest son of the late John Boyd. In memory of his dear father, who passed away on 7th April 1943, at the age of forty-nine.

Your father's time has come, Rabbie,
To leave all earthly woe,
As was the Covenant, he is gone,
The way all flesh must go.
Bereavement visits every home
Tho' much we dread its call
There's none escape the penalty
Of our first parent's fall.

His death to you and me, Rabbie
Means just to pass away
And be forgotten, ere his bones
Have mixed in kindred clay.
But where there's neither sin nor pain
To taint unending bliss,
Believers' souls, thro' faith enjoy
Eternal happiness.

The grave is not the end, Rabbie,
Beyond there's life and light,
A home where beauty knows no bounds,
A land that knows no night.
From thence the Blest Redeemer came
And died to set us free
Lest we should perish as we ought
For our iniquity.

Yet often we forget, Rabbie,
That day at Calvary,
Sometimes we even dare to doubt
His Glorious Majesty,
But if it be His will to smite,
'Tis also His to save
He only takes in mercy
That which in His love He gave.

A Midnight Melody

Our hearts were bright
On Christmas night
We had such jolly fun
  We danced awhile
  In old-time style
Then ate the Christmas bun.

But all this time
Amid the swine
Apart from this an' these
  A sow hersell
  Gave birth to twall
Wee piggy, wiggy wees.

That night I sat
And things looked flat
I thought I'd have a chance
  To sing and shout
  An' act the nowt
Of course that's nothin' strange.

The oul hens danced
The wee calves pranced
To me this yielded joy
  They burled like wheels
  When I played reels
An' waltzed to "Sonny Boy".

But three or four
Oul' ducks next door
To this they did rebel
  The music's charm
  Had done them harm
This didn't please me well.

The rest rejoiced
At what I voiced
An' made these four surrender
  The oul' goose sang
  Till the rafters rang
And polka'd wi' the gander.

The night it passed
The pigs thrived fast
Their skins like first class silk
  They hae her tits
  Near tore tae bits
Applying for their milk.

The sow's no cross
Altho' she's boss
O' such an awkward squad
  She lets them fight
  Baith day and night
An' never says they're bad.

They might do well
Still one can't tell
The future of these pigs
  Sometimes they die
  I don't know why
But it's not by dancing jigs.

When murdered fat
An' put in sa't
They taste the mouth of man
  You know it's nice
  To get a slice
O' bacon in the pan.

I'll stop my lies
Till the breakfast fries
An' the teapot starts tae boil
  For folks must rise
  That's kind of wise
An' start their daily toil.

When I get fed
I'll go to bed
An' sleep this good God's day
  An' I'll need a shake
  For I'm hard to wake
From a "Midnight Melody".

A Poacher's Lament

'Tis help, dear Clergy, min' you're needin'
To soothe those hearts that noo are bleedin'
Since all your feelings, loves and cares
Flew out in sympathy for hares
Pray what has made your souls sae saft
An' in a twingling drive you daft
Perhaps your proposition has
The flavour of a goodly cause.

But worst of all you're kind o' late
The jolly sportsman's fun to hate
To save and spare that tail-less beast
That once was meant for man a feast
Say, what of those that now are killed?
An' many an' empty belly filled
Was not their skin as sweet to save
As those that we at present have.

Hares long ago were ranked as game
Now, why not let them be the same
They were I think as clever then
An' e'en as clever holy men
For, from the pulpit they would preach
On how the Heavens we might reach
But now the big half o' the sermon
Alludes to fish and fowl and vermin
Yet what the congregation want
It is the Parson's place to grant
But does a man's "Eternal End"
On such a stupid thing depend
Nay, surely men have purer views
Than worship God through hares and grews.

So dry your tear-stained saintly faces
An' pay attention to your places
For if you're meant for God's reflector
Then on God's glory why not lecture?
Instead the church you're just disgracing
By lecturing on greyhound racing
I think wi' that you shouldn'y bother
But feed your flocks on better fother
Give wholesome food, should they detest it
You pour it out, let them digest it.

Now to conclude, I'll say by jove
If clergymen can preach to prove
That wi' my greyhoun' I'm unholy
I'll kill the brute, an' keep a collie.

On a Victim of Scarlet Fever

Sore was the stroke that smote my heart
   When one that I know well
Beneath misfortune's cruel smart
   A helpless victim fell.

So sorrow throws its gloomy shade
   O'er those who love her best
Till she enjoys the health and peace
   She previously possessed.

Through each perplexing path of life
   Where troubles seldom cease
It seems the best are most exposed
   To danger and disease.

For should the fairest be preserved
   From fever or from chill
I know that Elsie never would
   Have suffered any ill.

The Tryst

First I meant to come and find you
  Then I thought I'd write instead
Just a sentence to remind you
  I'll be true to what I said.

What was sworn and sealed on Sunday
  By that treaty I abide
To be out on Easter Monday
  Sporting on the Collin side.

Where the breeze bestirs the heather
  How I'm longing to be there
Living for a day together
  Far from scenes of toil and care.

Should your boss your leave refuse you
  Or your parents call you home
For such reasons I'll excuse you
  Tho' I would that you could come.

For without you o'er the mountain
  I've a notion I would be
Like a ship without its captain
  Roaming on a lonesome sea.

So no matter, or whatever
  If you can, or cannot go
Do to me at least this favour
  Drop a line and let me know.

"Mrs Mckintyre goes to kirk'

Mrs McIntyre Goes To Kirk

In a country village long ago
  'Way north of Ballystone
There lived a Mrs McIntyre
  And John her little son.

One Sunday she desired to be
  Amongst the goodly few
To hear the truths that pass between
  The pulpit and the pew.

So John agreed to stay at home
  And do the household work
And mind the broth, while mother went
  To worship in the Kirk.

With huge supplies of sticks and peats
  He kept the fire aflame
'Till finally he could scarcely see
  The pot for reek and steam.

Here Johnnie thought 'twas mebbe time
  To gie the stuff a stir
But what he saw inside near changed
  The colour of his hair.

The sheep's head circling round the pot
  With jaws set wide ajar
The cloth had also been released
  And left the dumplin bare.

In horror Johnnie dropped the lid
  His face at once grew pale
And off he scampers to the church
  As hard as he could whail.

With breathless haste he passed the door
  And hurried down the aisle
Observing not the sexton's scowl
  Nor the parson's vacant smile.

"Oh, Mother, Mother, come at once"
  Was all that he could say
The mother made a facial sign
  For him to go away.

"The oul ewe's head," he shouts again
"It must be off its dot
It's chasing turnips, spuds and peas
Like vengeance through the pot.

"In fact its murderous onslaught
Has everything excited
And the dear old apple dumplin'
Has aff her shirt to fight it."

A Prayer for Jack

O Thou, most gracious and everlasting God, Creator and Governor of all things, in whose divine presence even the angels veil their faces and cry 'unclean', humbly we bow our heads before Thee in prayer, to ask for comfort and solace to Him who is laid on a bed of pain. Do Thou the Great Physician who, in the days of Calvary, went about giving sight to the blind and healing the poor of all manner of sickness, visit him in this dark hour, and if it be Thy will make him whole again, that he may enjoy the blessings of health, and see once more the fresh green fields and the beauty of the countryside. But if he must for a season suffer and endure the affliction of physical agony – have mercy on him, Lord, and in Thy loving kindness give him power and strength to bear. Or if it be Thy holy will, that he Thy servant must go down into the Valley of the Shadow of Death, do not forsake him, but let Thy Holy Spirit comfort him and abide with him, until at last by Thy grace we shall be united once again in the House of many Mansions, prepared for God's elect, before the foundation of the world, where neither sickness nor pain shall have dominion over us. All that we ask is in the name of Jesus, Thy Son and our Redeemer, to whom be all honour and glory ascribed, World without end,
Amen.

A Child

Wee helpless, senseless infant bud
　Of frail humanity
So full of earthly loveliness
　Yet void of vanity.

Sure I could pity thee, unlearned
　In love and happiness
So ignorant and unconcerned
　In everything that is.

Yet thou art blest in thy estate
　On this bleak world of woe
For thou can'st feel the scourge of fate
　Nor sorrow's piercing throe.

No wreckless passion tears thy breast
　No horror haunts thy mind
No dire despair disturbs thy rest
　Nor care of any kind.

Oh would, if such were so designed
　I were a child like thee
No wonder Jesus felt inclined
　To take them on His knee.

So innocent and pure at heart
　Endowed with sinless bliss
I'm sure in heaven you claim a part
　For such that kingdom is.

But are thou wise concerning such
　To know that truth divine
Is not my education much
　More profitable than thine?

Nay, if our knowledge we compare
　You're just as wise as me
For ere my soul can enter there
　I must as humble be.

The Holy Land

As all the earth from pole to pole
   We're welcome to espy
'Tis my desire to emigrate
   And quench my thirsty eye.

How sweet 'twould be to cross the sea
   And roam 'neath foreign skies
And see the various sights and scenes
   That charm the wanderers' eyes.

But still I think the best of all
   The rambles I have planned
Would be a journey to the East
   To see the Holy Land.

Where patriarchs and prophets lived
   Much more the Son of God
I'd love to be where He has been
   And tread where He has trod.

I think I'd start from Bethlehem
   The city of His birth
And walk in order as He walked
   When He was here on earth.

And see the city where He preached
   The garden where He prayed
The hill where He was crucified
   The tomb where He was laid.

All these, and many other sights
   Would lull my mind to rest
And quench the fire of keen desire
   That burns within my breast.

So should the journey come to pass
   That I intend some day
May He, who walked that way before
   Be with me on my way.

The Shepherd and His Sheep

(or 2nd Ballyeaston Choir)

There's nought can please the shepherd more
  Than hear his sheep rejoice
Each bleating forth, its note of praise
  According to its voice.

A perfect blend of tone and trend
  He does not ask to hear
The well meant murmurs, sighs and groans
  Are music to his ear.

Yet oft' the various keys and tones
  In scrieving discords rent
As piercing notes from loyal throats
  Mysteriously ascend.

Tho' we selected from the flock
  With talent more supreme
Don't sing the sacred melodies
  More worthy of esteem.

But this a duty we must do
  To learn the hymns and psalms
Then gladly raise the songs of praise
  Amongst the ewes and lambs.

'Tis meet for us to glorify
  The tender Shepherd's name
And never cease to thank Him for
  The mercies we obtain.

For we should ever bear in mind
  That we a wicked race
Are like the wretched prodigal
  Unworthy of His grace.

Yet though we've sinned and gone astray
  And did the Shepherd wrong
If by repentance we return
  He'll hearkin' to our song.

And take us from a cold domain
Of poor, unhealthy dells
And lead us to the richer plain
Where peace and plenty dwells.

That we His sheep may always graze
Where greenest pastures grow
And be convenient to a stream
Where quiet waters flow.

Where neither fox nor wolf corrupt
Nor dangerous serpents creep
But just the two inhabitants
The Shepherd and His sheep.

So let the multitude write
In music loud and long
Let praise impart, from every heart
And every voice be song.

To a Sister with a Xmas Card

Here is a little Xmas card
Upon this Xmas time
You see to imitate a bard
I put it into rhyme.

I haven't much to send you
More than I've said above
Except to give or lend you
A brother's warmest love.

To say I sent it sure I'm mad
You have it day by day
And will forever, as you had
Before you went away.

I hope you still have some for me
But keep some for some other
And I'll remain, content to be
Your biggest bletherin' brother.

The Potter and the Clay

When God the Potter takes the clay
His power is so divine
He shapes the vessel as He may
To suit His wise design.

No matter how it looks or lives
'Twas His to fore-ordain
For this His holy word declares
He fashioned none in vain.

So each and everyone is formed
To walk as He has willed
An' thus continually, until
His purpose is fulfilled.

And none can say "What does't thou?"
"Why hast thou made me thus?"
For as his will is done in Heav'n
'Tis also done with us.

We may incline to claim, we have
What freedom we require
To pick, an' choose, our ways and views
An' do as we desire.

Oh yes, 'tis true, but what we do
Is what the Lord allows
And everything that we receive
He willingly bestows.

He rules and regulates the world
Directing from His throne
He gives no reason for His ways
But says – "As it is done".

Had we the power to perceive
How He his works unite
We'd be like Christ, His only Son
As equal infinite.

But He the "God of every God"
In whom all hope relies
Had thought it good to keep such things
Concealed from mortal eyes.

So naught the carnal mind conceives
Of holy intellect
But "Faith" – a gift He freely gives
Unto his own elect.

In whom He plants the seed of life
That they may understand
And with their souls effectually
His Spirit corresponds.

To them He says, "Be not afraid"
Believe that "I am He"
For on the Cross at Calvary
I bled and died for thee.

Then when the time appointed comes
He calls them to the skies
To occupy that place prepared
For them in Paradise.

There with the Holy Host of Heaven
To bless the Trinity
With everlasting songs of praise
Throughout Eternity.

Appeals from the Church

I've just received your last report
Demanding urgent cash support
A cheque you claim the only option
To parish sale or public auction.
By what you say, there seems no doubt
The Church is almost down and out.
And very few will be surprised
The way affairs are organised
For when we all do meet to pray
Will soon be when we meet to pay.
And yet it seems the more you get
You sink the deeper into debt,
I wonder will it ever end
This rash, compulsory urge to spend,
Between repairs and renovations
And endless lists of alterations.
It's difficult to name them all
But here's a few I can recall,
The dome was doomed to rot and rust
The pulpit plagued with damp and dust
Then more requests for more donations
For light and heating installations
Then verily to crown them all
Extension to the lecture hall
For years the management could cope
With just the freewill envelope.
Except, perhaps on odd occasions
When by the preacher's smooth persuasions
A hardy hearer searched his purse
And smiled to hide a smothered curse.
The ten pound note now rules the fold
The Ten Commandments once controlled,
As time goes by the fashions change
And older people think it strange –
The temple treasury must have enough
Enough to make a golden calf.

"the Popes visit to Ireland"

The Pope's Visit to Ireland

Wee Eddie Adair, better known as Ned,
Of Protestant parents was born and bred,
A man with a passion for new Orange Halls,
Where he sang the come-all-yees at meetings and balls,
For Ned was an Orangeman, body and soul,
Wi' a temper and tongue that were hard to control.
He would fight, as they say, at the drop o' a hat
And the Pope was the boy he was aye wantin' at,
Yet he drank wi' his Catholic neighbours in pubs,
An' helped them to harvest their barley an' spuds,
But he wouldn'y be seen at their functions or feasts
For he niver could stomach the bishops and priests.

When he heard that the Pope was to visit the South,
He cursed ivery chapel, from Limerick to Louth,
And the clergy who canvassed for all they were worth
To have him persuaded to come to the North,
For surely like Herod, the Pope has been toul
That Ulster is waiting for Paisley or Powell
To find them the son of an English lord
Of the house and the lineage of William the 3rd.

Tormented wi' troubles so near to the Twelfth,
Religion and politics went for his health.
So the doctor advised him to rest for a spell,
To lie and relax and luk after hissel'.

As he hung up his sash on the en' o' the bed,
A plan for reprisal came into his head.
He'd go ower the border an' join in the mass
An' kick the oul Pope if he happened to pass.
"I'll lame him," says Ned, "Should I walk to Tralee
Or wherever the divil he happens to be,"
And to see the Pope limpin' would answer the prayers
Of ten generations of Eddie Adairs.

When he got to the place the parade had begun,
So he joined the procession disguised as a nun.
With the multitude chanting hosanna to Rome,
For a moment he thought that the Kingdom had come.

He had pictured his Holiness haggard and frail
Wi' a mantle to cover his horns and his tail,
But instead, there stood smiling and waving his han'
A healthy goodlukin' big lump o' a man
An' the way he appealed to the Provos to cease
An' live with their Protestant brithers in peace
Ned thumped an oul priest on the back, and says he –
"He's less o' a Fenian than Thomas O'Feigh."

Back home at his farm on an Antrim hill,
His mother has doubts about peace and goodwill
There's so much religion, she can't understand,
Why heathens inherit this beautiful land.
It seems such a pity, the Pope and the Prod
Are rinnin' in different directions to God,
They have so much in common, including their Faith
And Ireland has always had room for them baith.

A Meditation

Such was the lot of fallen man
Since Adam disobeyed
That he must toil his kindred soil
To earn his daily bread.

Not to depend upon his friend
Nor trust it to his neighbour
But plough, an' sow, and hoe and mow
And live by honest labour.

I, to the fact can witness bear
For this is my occupation
As I've been born a farmer's heir
And doomed to cultivation.

From dawn to dark I do my work
To win what I require
Though I possess no more, but less
Than what I might desire.

No wage I get, or have as yet
Outside my father's fields
But roughly clad, and plainly fed
From what my labour yields.

Tho' oft' I've tried an' oft applied
For a better situation
But something aye stood victor by
To conquer my ambition.

It seems that fortune places strife
Where natural crave inclines
And both together guide a life
As Providence designs.

I mind, I used to think this world
A rich and rare dominion
But, oh, these few short years of time
Have altered my opinion.

At first when my existence dawned
Enwrapped in prosperous guise
Bright hues of fortune's fairest sun
Bedecked the eastern skies.

On the Death of a Sister

Through many a long and lonesome hour
The night of sorrow reigned
While slowly death's consuming power
Its bleak intentions gained.

But like the awakening dawn of day
That sheds the gloom apart
So shone the bright, redeeming ray
Upon the dying heart.

When doctor's skilful aid had failed
To soothe her ceaseless pain
She turned to Heaven and cried, where cry
Was never heard in vain.

And God set free that fettered soul
And took it up above
Where sleep is blessed with endless dreams
Of happiness and love.

Then tell her parents not to weep
Nor should they be distressed
When Jesus plucked the flower, He meant
To wear it in His breast

And they through faith by heaven's grace
Shall join her by and by
Where God for aye shall wipe away
The tear from every eye

A Prayer

To Thee above, oh Heavenly Father
My humble prayer ascends,
As on Thy ever present aid
My weary soul depends.

I come before Thee through the One
Who died that we might live
To beg from Thee necessities,
That Thou alone can'st give.

If Thou would'st scorn my low estate
Or brush my pleas aside
What other source could I approach
In whom I might confide.

For none my final destiny
Hath power to control
But Thou, the Author of my flesh
And pilot of my soul.

When dark and dangerous enemies
Their threatening woes proclaim
The Holy Spirit quickens me
To call upon Thy name.

Tho' great and many are the gifts,
And blessings I receive
It seems my thankless being fails
Their greatness to perceive.

I know that I should worship Thee
With reverence and respect
Yet, I, oh Lord, concerning Thee
My duties oft' neglect.

For towards temptations luring sweet
I naturally incline
When evil powers becken me
To stray from Thee and Thine.

But Thou, Almighty King of Kings
Forgive my vain desires
And shed abroad the cleansing balm
My sinful soul requires.

With not a sign of sorrow seen
But pleasure leaning toward me
I thought life could, and surely would
Abundantly reward me.

But now the veil is rent aside
Those longed for things have fled
I now behold a world that's cold
Where sorrows reign instead.

Alas, too true that promised joys
Are hopeless expectations
And infant schemes like idle dreams
Are vain imaginations.

Then bless'd are they who don't expect
To be by luck annointed
At fortune frown they're not cast down
Nor sadly disappointed.

So I shall learn to thank the Lord
For all that He bestows me
And thus content myself henceforth
With what His law allows me.

From paths of selfishness and sin
Be pleased to set me free
And make me more and more to walk
In fellowship with Thee.

That I may daily find delight
Obeying Thy command
And when Thy spirit soothes or chides
I'll feel and understand.

So God as Thou hast been my guide
Be Thou my Guardian still
And deal with me continually
According to Thy will.

May this my humble prayer be heard
And answered through Thy love
And may Thy name be loved below
As it is blessed above.

All that I ask, O Heavenly Father
I ask in Jesus' name
Who was and is and aye shall be
For evermore – Amen.

A Toast

As a toast to the future of bridegroom and bride
On behalf of the couple who stood by their side
For better for worse, whatever betide
We'll always remember the knot being tied.

Well Robert had sworn he must have a wife
Regardless of rations or national strife
So the wee Guy Macbeth, wi' a voice like a fife,
From a sentence of scripture, gave a sentence for life.

We know that as lovers they always agreed
As husband and wife may they also succeed
And when age has deprived them of beauty and speed
May they still be companions, the comfort they need.

For Robert's a buddy baith dacent and square,
And Marie's a woman as good as she's fair,
United as one, may that one be a pair
Who will always have plenty, and plenty to spare.

So we'll pray that they never get married again
While they have each other and a hame o' their ain
To cherish and honour thro pleasure and pain
Forsakin all others, forever Amen.

A Letter to Ray in Southport

Dear Sister

Once more I send a line or two
Across the Irish Sea to you
I'm sure you're glad to hear frae hame
If I was there, I'd be the same.

Well round about, there's little strange
Except the gossip often change
The folk just keep up idle crack
Behin' some decent body's back
It des'ny tak' sae' much to happen
Tae' cause debate, an' keep them yappin'
When e'er they hear o' some misdeed
Their tongues are aff at "Bluebird" speed
They hae somethin' new wi' ivery breath
A birth, a marriage or a death.

There's some half glad, an' some half bargy
About the parting wi' the clergy
The Reverend Harrison (William John)
Has from his congregation gone
To shed his godliness abroad
To criminals up the Crumlin Road
Last Sunday night the folk went swarmin'
To hear him preach his farewell sermon
An' min' ye, it was nae' bare whistle
For he can fairly phrase the gospel.
He took his text: John Chapter VII
An' settled on verse thirty seven
Look up that place and read that same
For sure 'twould bate me tae' explain
You'll see the text wi' him just fitted
His last one here before he flitted.

Well now to change the subject roun'
An' turn the topics up and down
I'm goin' to Larne to take my place in
The "Country Fiddlers" competition
I'll ha'e ta'e tune my fiddle up
An' bid for brave "Lord Antrim's Cup"
At clear tone concert pitch I'll set her
Then do my best, or even better

Ould reels an' hornpipes are requested
An' that's the yins that I'm the best at
Of course at Larne it might be awkward
I'll no can play, I'll be that backward
But to be present is well worth while
To see an' hear the good oul style
I'll write and let you know the winner
Should he or she be saint or sinner.

I think that's a' I ha'e tae scribble
Except some yarns no worth the trouble
This leaves me well, in health the best
A' one, O.K. an' all the rest
Well that's the lot at present handy
So goodbye, Ray, write soon, from Sandy.

P.S.
Please excuse my grammar, smashes,
Mistakes, strokes, commas,
Dots and dashes.

To James McCrory – Canada

(5 November 1931)

I now my pen and page prepare
  My conscience to obey
So, Jammie, please for old times' sake
  Excuse my long delay.

Each day since I received your note
  To write I did intend
Accept the lame apology
  I so sincerely send.

I love to correspond with friends
  Who roam in distant climes
And hear results of how they fare
  Through these uncertain times.

D'ye min' the nights we used to spend
  Wi' games and tricks galore
An' dancing wi' the big nailed boots
  'Till we near smashed the floor.

An' Houston Dempsey took the bun
  He fairly styled himsel'
He thought his fiddle must be Stradds
  An' he, a perfect swell.

He sa'd an' thra'd like somethin' mad
  Wi' an' awkward, artless wrist
His hame constructed instruments
  Got many an' ugly twist.

He's greatly changed, but for the worse
  His e'en gets like a griddle
An' faith he seems to lose control
  O' fingers, face an' fiddle.

Well, James, the harvest season's past
  The win' blaws bleak an' thin
And once again, the scanty grain
  Is safely gathered in.

I hope your form keeps feeling fit
  Your heart a gleesome tone
For mind a dull, unhappy soul
  Is apt to dry the bone.

Besides the strife we meet in life
  Our hearts betimes grow tender
There's many a happy hour spent
  Among the weaken gender.

Have you yet met the charming dame
  That's goin' to be your bride?
To keep you warm throughout the storm
  An' lay your cares aside.

They say there's love wi' married life
  Then may you live to share it
And may your burden aye be light
  Your back aye fit to bear it.

An Apology Enclosed with a Pair of Lady's Dancing Shoes

Excuse and pardon me, Dear Mae,
  My memory's so disbanding
Our theory was mismanaged for
  A lack of understanding.

Should I have kept your dancing wear
  An' been the "noble fellow"
And made once real, the fairy tale
  Of the Prince and Cinderella.

Ah, nay no hurried links we'll lock
  In case we couldn't bear them
So I return your shoes with care
  For faith I couldn't wear them.

A Consoling Recitation

I feel as if I owe thee much
For thy consoling, friendly touch
No doubt you're worthy of my credit
For what you said, an' how you said it.

In truth, I used to wonder oft
If bands and minstrels went aloft
Especially me, I had my doubts
Of my eternal whereabouts.

But since I heard your recitation
Each line a phase of consolation
I can't express the way it pleased me
Nor yet describe how much it eased me.

'Twas like a weight rolled off my chest
That long my tender crappin' pres't
What better news could I be given
Than hear that fiddlers go to Heaven.

Of course I knew that Psalmist David
How he made songs and sung and raved
Then, when his wild career ended
He toward the sky abode ascended
But min' wi' me I don't compare him
A saint beside a "Herrim-Skerrim".

Yet I'll complete that upward journey
Providing Peter desn'y turn me
Where I can get a harp to strum-on
To practise for the "Kingdom comin".

But here remember wantin' jokin'
I didn'y mean tae be provokin
I would be loath to mock salvation
Our only hope from condemnation.

Still we're commanded to be merry
To wait, to trust, but never worry
Then let's of life its best enjoy
That's all, from yours, "The Minstrel Boy".

A Bereavement

Death unexpected came
  Driving us wild
Taking them both at once
  Mother and child.
Shadowed by sorrow's power
  Smote in her hopeful hour
Also the infant flower
  Tender and mild.

Tho' in the strangers' eyes
  Sad as it seems
None but the near bereaved
  Know what it means
Yet God had thought it best
  Nearer the Saviour's breast
Where in His home of rest
  Love ever reigns.

We would not grieve so sore
  Could we but see
Those that have gone before
  Are happier than we
There in a land so fair
  Safe with the Master there
Far from all kinds of care
  Happy and free.

Slowly the time draws nigh
  When we shall see
With them and Thee on high
  Lord may we be.
So while we yet remain
  May thou our faith sustain
That we may still obtain
  Mercy from Thee.

To a Robin

Poor wee innocent bird
You look frightfully scared
Sure you needn't be shy or alarmed
If the storm and the sleet
Has deprived you of heat
You were right to come in and get warmed.

There's a shelter from cold
For the sparrow I'm told
And the swallow hath also a nest
And I'm sure there's a spot
Meant for thee and the lot
By that sacred sign on thy breast.

Did you see I was ill
As you sat on the sill
Then you entered as quick as you could
To apply a first aid
Like your forefathers did
When they buried the babes in the wood.

Well, I'm thankful indeed
For your offer in need
To assist me was thoughtful of you
But for me being dead
Never bother your head
For I've got a touch of the 'flu.

You're as welcome to stay
As the flowers of May
But of care you would lessen my load
If you swiftly resign
From this prison of mine
To your humble but peaceful abode.

For if Sadie arrives
I could bet both our lives
You'll be wishing you'd stayed in the hedge
For no matter how fast
Or how cruel the blast
It could never compete with her rage.

Now, since I've took to bed
It's with hens I've been fed
That have suffered for years with the croup
And if she gets her hands
On your feathery glands
I will shortly be supping your soup.

Then at such an affair
All the fowls of the air
Will be falling a-sighing and sobbin'
So for my sake, take care
Lest I witness must bear
To the death of their dearest, Cock Robin.

A Prayer

Almighty Lord of Love and Life
 And God for evermore
Thy merciful forgiveness
 I earnestly implore.

Here as I lay me down to sleep
 Let angels watch my rest
And soothe the restless woes and pains
 That strive within my breast.

I need Thee every passing hour
 To bear my agonies
In joy, in sorrow, life and death
 Be with me, Lord, always.

When I approach the yawning grave
 And death stands victor by
Be pleased to quicken me, that I
 May feel Thy presence nigh.

In that dread hour, thro' death's dark vale
 Conduct me with thy grace
And make my soul presentable
 Before Thy Father's face.

For, lo, if I be left alone
 Where would my spirit go
Would not my sinful soul be doomed
 To everlasting woe.

But with my trembling hand in Thine
 Why should I be afraid
When for eternal life by Thee
 The ransom has been paid.

Then, Master, if it be Thy will
 My feeble faith sustain
And make me conscious as I pray
 I do not trust in vain.

Nor do I pray, because I fear
 The promise insecure
But just to make my calling safe
 And my election sure.

So may both Heaven and Earth combine
   And bless Thy holy name
And may the glory all be Thine
   For evermore, Amen.

To My Father On His Death Bed

How soon we speel the allotted span
Of three score years and ten
A child, a youth, a full grown man,
Then like a child again
We lose our grip on worldly fare
And grope for the hand that will lead us, where
The near and future blend in one
And whatsoever is willed is done.

A feeble form, a weary brain
A soul by age matured;
The Reaper stoops to lift the grain
He by his death secured.
For this is the lot of the human race
That here there is no abiding place
And all who come must pass away
For none has ever come to stay.

Then gone . . . And soon to be forgot
Except by those concerned
The door is shut and what we owe
Can never be returned.
The bed of soil will soon erode
The temple where the soul abode,
And all that's left when we have fled,
Is what we did, and what we said.

Jean

Jean

(Died on the 20th April 1972)

I walk in the shadow of sorrow today
The light of my life has been taken away
And I can't find a reason why God should decree
That this thing should happen to Jeanie and me.

We were always together, and while she was spared
Our days were enriched by the pleasures we shared,
The flowers, the sunsets, the tints on a tree
Were glimpses of heaven to Jeanie and me.

The ties of affection and friendship we knew
Became closer and stronger the older we grew
For twenty-one years we were happy and free
And fortune looked kindly on Jeanie and me.

But now that I've lost her I feel so alone
No tongue could interpret the anguish I've known
There's little but grief in the future I see
Since death put a screen between Jeanie and me.

Beyond the horizon of death and the grave
There's a place for the sinner Christ promised to save
Prepared in that Mansion, wherever it be
Perhaps there's a place for Jeanie and me.